EASY REFERENCE GUIDE TO
BREAKING
STRONGHOLDS

REBECCA GREENWOOD

DESTINY IMAGE® PUBLISHERS, INC.

P.O. Box 310, Shippensburg, PA 17257-0310

"Promoting Inspired Lives."

This book and all other Destiny Image and Destiny Image Fiction books are available at Christian bookstores and distributors worldwide.

Cover design by Eileen Rockwell

Interior design by Terry Clifton

For more information on foreign distributors, call 717-532-3040.

Reach us on the Internet: www.destinyimage.com.

ISBN 13 TP: 978-0-7684-5847-3

ISBN 13 eBook: 978-0-7684-5848-0

For Worldwide Distribution, Printed in the U.S.A.

1 2 3 4 5 6 7 8/24 23 22 21 20

How Are Strongholds Established?

"How are strongholds established?" The truth is the enemy has never, nor will he ever, play fair. He can and does set up traps in our lives. Those traps, in turn, cause us to be in bondage to a stronghold in our minds, thoughts, emotions, and spiritual lives. The traps that lead us into bondage can include trauma, betrayal, abuse, rejection, abandonment, accidents, bullying, ungodly control, angry family members, and so on.

A second avenue by which strongholds can be established is through what is termed a generational iniquity or also stated generational curse. Exodus 20:4–6 explains:

> No carved gods of any size, shape, or form of anything whatever, whether of things that fly or walk or swim. Don't bow down to them and don't serve them because I am God, your God, and I'm a most jealous God, punishing the children for any sins their parents pass on to them to the third, and yes, even to the fourth generation of those who hate me. But I'm unswervingly loyal to the thousands who

love me and keep my commandments (The Message).

The actual Hebrew word used in this scripture for *sin* is *avown*. It is translated "iniquity, guilt, a judicial state of being liable for a wrong done." When past generations in our family line have worshiped idols, turned their backs on God, hated God, sinned repeatedly or have been bound in addictions, etc., these sinful choices and activities will open a door for strongholds to be passed down the family line. The good report is that through Jesus we have forgiveness, grace, and mercy: "His mercy extends to those who fear him, from generation to generation" (Luke 1:50). Therefore, we can repent of the sin in the generational family bloodline, be set free from its demonic grip, and provide a righteous inheritance for ourselves and the generations to come.

A third way strongholds can become established in our lives is by willful sin we actively choose to engage in. When we sin and continually fall prey to repeated sin patterns, we give the enemy access to our personal lives, our thought lives, our emotions, our spiritual life, and even our physical bodies. In Ephesians 4:27 Paul instructs us to "Leave no [such] room or foothold for the devil [give no opportunity to him]" (AMPC).

The Greek word for *foothold* in this verse is *topos*. It is defined: "place, location, region, room, opportunity." When we sin, we give the devil an opportunity to invade our lives as well as our thoughts, emotions, physical bodies, and those areas in which we carry influence. Therefore, he establishes a demonic grip of bondage. To have victory, we must be intentional in choosing to let go of old sinful patterns and embracing and walking in the new nature available to us through Jesus. It is a must that we set our minds, wills, emotions, and actions on choosing this pursuit of holiness, seeking the Lord and His ways, and cultivating a spiritual lifestyle for awesome divine encounters with God that will bring transformation.

Prayer of Repentance and Renunciation

For further guidance in this process, take time to review the demonic strongman list in this book. Ask the Holy Spirit to reveal areas where you need freedom.

Father, I rejoice in the fact that Your truth sets me free. I welcome Your delivering anointing to envelop me now. Holy Spirit, guide me in this time of prayer and highlight to me those areas in which

I need to repent. [Allow the Holy Spirit to reveal to you every sin, sinful thought pattern, and stronghold that has gripped your mind, emotions, actions, life. Do not rush this process. When you are ready, engage in a time of confession and repentance.]

I confess that I (or my past generations) have been involved in the sin of _____ [specifically name the sins] *and we have embraced stronghold of* _____ [specifically name the strongholds that have gripped your family line and life].

Thank You, Lord, that in You we have redemption and through Your blood the forgiveness of sins. Thank You that Your blood is greater and more powerful than any of my mistakes and sins. You have come to rescue me from the enemy's hand. Jesus, I bring these issues to You, and I repent of them now. I ask that You forgive me for them.

I renounce, break, and cancel all activity of the stronghold of _____ [specifically name the stronghold]. *I speak to this stronghold and say that your hold is broken off of my family line, on my father's side and mother's side all the way back to Adam and Eve. I say right now that you are evicted out of my life and the lives of my children and my children's children and generations to come. Your assignment and grip are cancelled now, in the name of Jesus. I am no longer submitted to you.*

I ask, Holy Spirit, that as I have been washed clean by Jesus's blood, You will fill my mind, thoughts, emotions, physical body, and life to over-flowing with life, love, patience, freedom, joy, purity, goodness, holiness, humility, righteousness, and acceptance [or all other suggested spiritual blessings listed under the stronghold in the grouping list] *as Your child. I rejoice in Your glorious freedom! In Jesus's name, amen.*

THE NECESSITY OF FORGIVENESS

In Matthew 6:14–15 Jesus says, "If you forgive other people when they sin against you, your heavenly Father will also forgive you. But if you do not forgive others their sins, your Father will not forgive your sins." When we confess our sins to God but do not forgive others, we are asking God to do something for us that we ourselves are not willing to do for others.

As we discuss forgiveness, there are two issues I want to quickly address. Often when individuals suffer through difficult and traumatic situations, they become angry with God. They blame Him for their pain, and they bring His goodness into question: "How could God allow this to happen? Why didn't He protect me?" The Bible teaches that we live in a fallen world. People sometimes make horrible decisions, especially those who have not received salvation. God is grieved when bad things happen to His children and when His children make tragic and harmful mistakes. Our heavenly Father is a loving God—His love is more immense than we can comprehend. It is important for us to realize that the bad things that occur in our lives are not God's fault. He is not the one to blame.

The other issue I would like to address is our need to forgive ourselves. Each of us has been affected by mistakes we have made that have led to anguish and loss. Even though these events cannot be wiped out, we can learn from the poor choices we have made, and those lessons can result in great maturity and spiritual growth. The problem is that we sometimes beat ourselves up and resist being set free from thoughts and feelings of guilt. The truth is, when Jesus hung on the cross, He forgave us of our sins. Our trespasses have been washed away by His blood, and they are completely removed from us as far as the north is from the south and the east is from the west—in other words, they are gone forever! If Jesus has forgiven us our mistakes; we should do the same.

A Prayer of Forgiveness

Lord, thank You for Your truth and for Your amazing love. I am so grateful for the price You paid on the cross for me and for every person who has ever lived. Thank You for forgiving my sins and bringing the gift of salvation into my life. It is Your truth and love that set me free.

I desire to walk as You walked—in a lifestyle of forgiveness. I confess that I have not been willing to release and to forgive some who have betrayed and disappointed me. But now, today, I make the choice to forgive each person who has treated me poorly, betrayed me, made false accusations against me, brought dishonor into my life, abused me, bullied me, or lied to me. [Name any other action done to you that has caused unforgiveness.] *I choose to forgive* _____ [name out loud anyone whom the Lord is showing you to forgive], *and I ask that You forgive this person (or these people).*

Lord, in every area of my life in which I have been angry with You, I ask that You forgive me. I choose to believe in Your goodness, truth, and love.

In every area of my life in which I have not forgiven myself, I choose right now to release myself. Lord, I know that You love me, and therefore I choose to love myself. I speak to you, unforgiveness and bitterness, and I say that in every place in which you have taken hold of my emotions, I cancel your hold now.

Father, Your Word tells us to bless those who persecute us, so now, Lord, I speak Your blessing to each person whom I have chosen to forgive. Lord, touch each one of them with Your Father's heart of love. Teach me to love with Your heart. Teach me how to emulate Your heart of mercy, grace, and forgiveness. In Jesus's name, amen.

SOUL TIES

The Bible tells us that the marriage bed is to be undefiled. Why is the Lord so clear about this in scripture? It is because the act of sex is not only a physical union but also a spiritual union. This union is meant to unite one man and one woman, consummating the covenant made before God in a marriage ceremony. The Lord designed sexual intimacy to be holy, pure, and treasured. It is in the secret and sacred place of the marriage bed that the part of ourselves created to be pure and set apart is given away and a spiritual and emotional tie is created.

Sadly, the defilement of the marriage bed has become commonplace in our society. Sexual sins such as promiscuity, fornication, adultery, homosexuality, pornography, lust, bestiality, prostitution, and other immoral acts have been embraced as an accepted part of culture. When these rebellious acts of sexual perversion are participated in, powerful doors to the demonic realm are opened and a spiritual and emotional connection known as a soul tie is formed between the individuals involved.

Soul ties are formed between those who jointly engage in sinful, ungodly activities and practices. They are also established in acts of violation and trauma in relationships based on ungodly control and unhealthy emotional attachments. Ungodly vows made between friends, such as the pricking of fingers and intermingling of blood, result in an unholy pact. There is also the exchange of necklaces, where one friend wears the word *best* and the other wears the word *friend*. Soul ties are easily formed between the generations in a family line if generational curses are not broken and cut off. Once a soul tie is established between two individuals, the demonic can transfer from one person to the other. In other words, if one of the participants struggles with a spirit of pride, this demon now has access to the other person. The result is double trouble.

Time to Break the Hold of Soul Ties

In order to see the soul ties broken you want to ensure you identify those with whom a soul tie has been established. It is important to be in a place where you can be quiet with no distractions. Have a piece of paper and a pencil ready. Invite the presence of Holy Spirit ask Him to guide you discerning those with whom an unholy soul tie has been formed. As the names come to mind, be sure to write them on the piece of paper. Once you feel the list is complete, it is now time to pray!

> Lord, I come before You and confess that in these relationships unholy soul ties have been formed. I confess this is a sin and I ask now, Lord, that You forgive me for all impure and unholy activities I engaged in and all emotional control I have given to those who should not have that influence in my life. Lord, I thank You for Your unending forgiveness and that these sins are washed clean by Your blood.

Now, in the name of Jesus, and by the authority He has bestowed to me, I cut and break all ungodly soul ties with past partners or husband/wife [name each of them] *who have been abusive, unholy, or illicit. All relationships in which emotional control has been established in my life, I cut and break all unholy soul ties. I sever physical, spiritual, and emotional ties with* _____

_____ [name all with whom you have been intimate or allowed to gain emotional control over you]. *I renounce and break all sexual relationships that were in disobedience to God and His Word. I command all strongmen and their demonic households to be broken, plundered, and destroyed in my life. I bind, gag, renounce, and evict all evil spirits that have been empowered by the soul ties and command all spirits transferred to me through these sinful actions and ungodly emotional associations to leave.*

All demons that gained access through these relationships, you are no longer welcome and I shut the door of access to my body, mind, thoughts, emotions, and desires. The open door of access is shut and sealed now through the blood of Jesus.

I declare by the authority of Jesus that all demons and demonic powers that have been cast out have no power over my family members or their children. Your assignment is cut off and cast out now in Jesus's name.

Holy Spirit, I now invite and welcome You to aid me in rebuilding and establishing righteous, pure, holy, and godly covenant ties in my life—relationships in alignment with Your perfect plan and design. I now call forth, welcome, and activate in my life the power of the cross, the blood of the Lamb, the resurrection life of Jesus, and the authority of being seated with Him in heavenly places and say that this is now activated and set against Satan's plans and schemes for me and my family. Thank you, Lord, that I am free and free indeed! I rejoice in this victorious moment of freedom in my life! It is Your name I pray, amen.

TRAUMA

Webster's New World Dictionary defines trauma as "a bodily injury, wound or shock; or a painful emotional experience or shock that often produces a lasting psychic effect." Experiencing trauma can have a powerful and formidable effect. As we grow, change, and have wide-ranging experiences throughout our lives, our beliefs and suppositions typically evolve over time. When we experience trauma, those beliefs and perceptions that help us make sense of the world around us change almost instantly. It is common for people to experience intrusive and disturbing thoughts, worry, difficulty sleeping, trouble focusing, bouts of crying, blame or self-judgment, and lack of satisfaction. The effects of trauma also can result in extreme emotional fluctuations, unhappiness, anxiety, loneliness, anger, irritability, and demonic harassment. Undergoing multiple traumas or repeatedly being exposed to life-threatening events can have a further unfortunate impact.

Even when we have no influence or control over a traumatic event that occurs in our lives, Satan sees our suffering as an open door to bring additional wounding in the form of tormenting thoughts. Please remember this: *Satan has never, nor will he ever, play fair!* He will take advantage of an unsettling experience to gain a foothold in our lives. It is in our times of pain and emotional distress that the enemy will fill us with thoughts of fear, confusion, anger, rejection, distrust, unbelief, victimization, and the like. Remember, the enemy can bring these thoughts to our minds and emotions, but a stronghold is established only if we get into a pattern of entertaining his lies. As these thoughts and attitudes take hold, we become bound by the tormenting event and often a resulting stronghold of trauma, rejection, victim spirit, fear, and depression. It's time to pray.

Lord, thank You for revealing to me the unhealed areas in my life. God, I welcome Your love and Your presence to embrace me now. Everyone who has brought hurt, pain, and trauma into my life through events in my past I choose to forgive now in Jesus's name [speak out the names of all those you are to release and forgive].

For every time and way in which I have questioned Your goodness and love and have blamed You, I ask that You forgive me. For every wrong belief or lie that I have embraced in my thought life and emotions, I ask Your forgiveness. I choose now to release myself from any and all anger, guilt, shame, and condemnation that I have heaped on myself. Jesus, Your blood sets me free. You have made a way for me to walk victoriously. I know that You love me.

So now I choose to break the power of all trauma in my thoughts and emotions. I cancel, in the name of Jesus, any and all rejection, fears, anxiety, confusion, lack of trust, and addictions [insert here any other issues that need to be spoken out loud in this prayer] *that have kept me bound.*

Lord, I now invite You to bring healing to my memories where each trauma occurred. I welcome Your healing touch and perfect love to touch every memory and that any and all pain or sting in the memory will be completely removed.

Lord, I thank You that You fill me with Your Spirit and Your love. I am Your child. You love me. I receive now the freedom and love that You have made available to me. Father, I say yes and amen to the plans and purposes that You have for my life. I believe that I am fearfully and wonderfully made. Your Word says that I am the head and not the tail. I speak to my mind and emotions to be full of joy, peace, comfort, love, patience, and long-suffering. I know that I am accepted and loved by You, Lord. I thank You, Lord, for this freedom from the pain of the past and that I am no longer bound. I rejoice in You and praise Your awesome, magnificent, and holy name. Amen.

Prayer to Plunder and Break the Strongman's Grip

Before we start this prayer, I want to begin with some instruction. You will refer to the strongman list to guide you in this prayer of deliverance and freedom. In this prayer we are going to bind the strongman and plunder its house, meaning all the activity of demons and evil it brings along with itself. Then we will evict the strongman. Why? We want to ensure that the strongman is totally disarmed and dismantled so complete freedom will come.

> *Spirit of* [name the strongman], *I bind and gag you and declare you powerless by the authority given to me in Jesus. Today I am taking authority over you and rendering you your eviction notice out of life, off of my mind and thought life, desires, physical body, and out of my emotions*
>
> *Now in the name of Jesus I command all* [begin to speak out one by one the activities and manifestations on the list. Following each manifestation or activity make the following declaration]. *I break your assignment and declare your power null and void. I command your hold is broken now in Jesus's name and I break you from the strongman of* [name the strongman].

All of the demonic activities and manifestations accompanying the demonic strongmen on the list are methodically prayed through. As you do this, freedom will come. Once the list has been prayed through in its entirety, move into evicting the strongman as directed below.

[Name the strongman], your house has been plundered. All spirits have been broken and given their eviction notice. Now in the name of Jesus, I command you [name the strongman] to get out now. I renounce and rebuke your power and say you are no longer welcome in my life. Get out now in the name of Jesus.

What you will find is the strongman will leave quickly and quietly because there is no ground holding it. Now fill up the empty house:

Lord, I praise You and rejoice that freedom has come into my life. I rejoice that my house has been swept clean and I ask that you now come and fill me up with Your presence. I speak and loose [name those things to be welcomed in and to be loosed into your life shared at the end of each strongman section]. Lord, fill me to overflowing, and seal the work that has been done here by the blood of the Lamb. I declare I am completely free in Jesus's name.

CLOSING AND BLESSING PRAYER

To be prayed following the cutting off and casting out of the strongman:

Father, thank You for touching my life and setting me free from the strongholds that have gripped me. You are an awesome, faithful, delivering God and I rejoice that the strongholds have been plundered and defeated and I am free.

I choose this day to encounter the mind of Christ. God, cause me to love what You love and to lead a lifestyle of love, compassion, holiness, humility, patience, and faithfulness. Lord, I commit to live a life based on Your truth, love, and grace. Cause me to hate evil and sin. Keep me from evil and its temptations. Holy Spirit, fill me up to overflowing. May I walk freely in Your Spirit and welcome a new move of Your love, anointing, grace, and authority to flow through my life.

Lord, I declare that from this day forward I will value what You value and live a victorious life as Your child. I delight in the truth that You have called me out of darkness and into Your marvelous light. Lord, I choose to take refuge in You. I choose to be glad and to sing for joy.

Spread Your protection over me. I love You and rejoice in Your name. Lord, bless me and surround me with Your favor as a shield. May I behold and experience You in new ways. I desire more of You, Jesus. Cause me to be transformed from glory to glory into Your image and to be a child who radiates You.

Lord, thank You that I am Your child. Lord, I rejoice that I am blessed with the healing of all wounds of rejection, neglect, and abuse. With a bubbling over peace—the peace that only the Prince of peace can give, a peace beyond comprehension. Thank You, Lord, for blessing me with a fruitful life—good fruit, much fruit, and fruit that remains. Thank You that I am blessed with the spirit of sonship and that I am a (son or daughter) of the King of kings. Thank You for the rich inheritance I have in Your kingdom.

I receive and rejoice that I am blessed though You with success. I am the head and not the tail, above and not below. Thank You for blessing me with health and strength of body, soul, and spirit. I welcome Your blessing of overflowing successfulness, enabling me to be a blessing to others. Awaken in me and through me the blessing of spiritual influence modeling that You are the light of the world and the salt of the earth. Lord, I thank You that Your Word declares that I am like a tree planted by rivers of water and that I will thrive in all Your ways.

I rejoice that I am blessed with a depth of spiritual understanding and an intimate walk with

You. I say that I will not stumble or falter, for Your Word will be a lamp to my feet and a light to my path. Lord, bless me with pure, edifying, encouraging, and empowering relationships in life. I receive the blessing of Your favor and that I walk in favor with You and man. I say I will walk in abounding love and life. I am blessed with power, love, and a sound mind. With wisdom from on high, I will minister God's comforting grace and anointing to others. Lord, thank You for the blessing and Kingdom inheritance I walk in as Your child! I am truly blessed with all spiritual blessings in Jesus. Amen!

APPARENT DEMONIC GROUPINGS LIST

SPIRIT OF ANTICHRIST

Everyone who does not acknowledge that Jesus is from God has the spirit of antichrist, which you heard was coming and is already active in the world (1 John 4:3).

Bind: *Spirit of Antichrist*

Plunder its house!

- Repentance for aligning with and operating under the influence of the spirit of antichrist
- Break attachments from the below listed activities and other partnering demonic spirits
- Renounce all of the following activities
- Cast out or evict all partnering evil spirits

Signs: *Self-Exalting, Humanism, Opposes Jesus, Critical, Confusion, Occult*

Attempts to Take Christ's Place

Blasphemes Holy Spirit

Displays Open Unbelief

Acts/Speaks Against

The miracles of God, Word of God, testimony of Jesus

Christ and His teachings, God, Christians

Denies/Opposes

Atonement of Christ, deity of Christ, humanity of
Christ, blood of Christ
Work of the Holy Spirit, ministry and victory of
Christ miracles

Rationalizes

Christ, the Word, miracles

Disturbs Fellowship and Gathering of the Saints

Stirs up strife between believers
Harasses, persecutes the saints
Suppresses ministry

Doctrinal Error/Twisting of Doctrine

Humanism
Legalism
Cults, Occult
Note: For *Cults* see also Familiar Spirit

Closed-Minded

Confusion

Deceiver

Defensiveness

Self-Exalting

Worldliness

Critical, Mocking Attitude

Judgmentalism

Lawlessness

Mean-spirited

Violent

Once the house is plundered: command the antichrist to get out.

- Issue an eviction notice to this spirit (Speak it out loud)
- Loose and welcome in: a dynamic personal relationship with Jesus, a baptism in the Holy Spirit, grace, truth, awakening to the Word of God, awakening to the presence of God, a hunger and faith to know Him more, spirit of prophecy, gift of teaching and sharing the true word of God, gifts of the Spirit

SPIRIT OF BONDAGE

Stand fast therefore in the liberty by which Christ has made us free, and do not be entangled again with a yoke of bondage (Galatians 5:1).

Bind: *Spirit of Bondage*

Plunder its house!

- Repentance for aligning with and operating under the influence of the spirit of bondage
- Break attachments from the below listed activities and other partnering demonic spirits
- Renounce all of the following activities
- Cast out or evict all partnering evil spirits

Signs: *Unworthiness, Rejection, Fears, Performance, Control, Pride, Self-Pity, Poverty Mindset, Feeling Lost, Addictions, Compulsions, Infirmity, Spiritual Oppression, Thoughts of Death*

Unworthiness/Worthlessness
Embarrassment, Shame, Condemnation, Rejection
Bruised Spirit, Anguish of Spirit, Brokenhearted
Self-Condemnation, Self-Pity

Bitterness/Resentment

Critical Spirit, Fault Finding, Judgmentalism, Accusation, Strife (conflict)

Self-Deception (believing what is not true about yourself, positive or negative)

Spiritual Blindness (inability to see God's truth)

Unrighteousness

Doubting salvation, no assurance of salvation, fear of death

Performance

Perfectionism, drivenness

False responsibility, false burden (not your own), false guilt

False compassion (misplaced compassion)

Anxiety, nervousness, frustration

Feeling Lost (disconnected)

Vagabond Spirit, Restlessness

Fears/Paranoia/Fear of Death

MPD (multiple personality disorder), Schizophrenia

Pride, Superiority

Control, Dominance, Possessiveness, Compulsory Subjection and Control, Slavery (enslavement, oppressed)

Poverty Mindset (never enough)/Coveting Wealth in Order to Hoard

Self-Reward

Compulsions and Addictions

Substances: Caffeine, cigarettes, alcohol, drugs (legal or illegal) or medications (beyond prescribed use)

Behaviors: Overeating (gluttony), anorexia, bulimia, overspending, sexual activity, overspending, addicted to working out, addicted to plastic surgery, addicted to altering one's body, addicted to television, addicted to online gaming, addicted to social media, fatal attraction, addicted to self-image, addicted to self-harm (cutting, embedding, bulimia, anorexia)

Unholy Soul Ties

Inability to Break Free/Bound

Helplessness, Hopelessness

Thoughts of Death, Death Wish, Thoughts/Attempts of Suicide

Phantom Pain (not due to loss of limb)

Infirmity

Stiffness

Chronic Fatigue

Idleness (sloth, sluggish)

Hyperactivity, ADD, ADHD

Tourette's Syndrome (involuntary activity, movements and vocalizations)

Spiritual Oppression

Mind Control

Witchcraft (rebellion)

Satanism

Once the house is plundered: command the spirit of bondage to get out.

- Issue an eviction notice to this spirit (Speak it out loud)
- Loose and welcome in: liberty, Spirit of Adoption, true kingdom identity, freedom and healing from all addictions, fresh infilling of the Holy Spirit

DEAF AND DUMB SPIRIT

Now when Jesus saw that the crowd was quickly growing larger, he commanded the demon, saying, "Deaf and mute spirit, I command you to come out of him and never enter him again!" (Mark 9:25)

Bind: *Deaf and Dumb Spirit*

Plunder its house!

- Repentance for aligning with and operating under the influence of the deaf and dumb spirit
- Break attachments from the below listed activities and other partnering demonic spirits
- Renounce all of the following activities
- Cast out or evict all partnering evil spirits

Signs: *Unforgiveness, Sorrow, Sleepiness, Confusion, Infirmity, Seizures, Accidents, Thoughts of Death*

Unforgiveness
Self-Pity/Wallowing/Pining Away
Uncontrolled Crying
Emotionless

Sleepiness

Confusion

Stuttering

Stupors (dazed)/Motionless Stupor

Lethargy (sluggish, slow)

Tourette's Syndrome

Chronic Infections

Chronic ear infections, eye diseases

Deafness/Blindness

Seizures

Convulsions, epilepsy, foaming at the mouth

Tearing Things, Gnashing of Teeth

Dumbness (insanity in the Greek)

Madness, insanity, lunatic behavior, schizophrenia

Poverty

Accidents

Burning accidents, drowning accidents, destruction
Fear of fire, fear of water

Thoughts of Death

Thoughts or acts of suicide, sensing approaching death

Death

Notes: For *Uncontrolled Crying* see also Spirit
of Heaviness

Once the house is plundered: command the deaf and dumb spirit to get out.

- Issue an eviction notice to this spirit
  (Speak it out loud)
- Loose and welcome in: healing, hearing, boldness, peace, deep and peaceful sleep

SPIRIT OF DEATH/SHADOW OF DEATH

Even though I walk through the valley of the shadow of death, I fear no evil, for You are with me; Your rod and Your staff, they comfort me (Psalm 23:4).

Bind: *Spirit/Shadow of Death*

Plunder its house!

- Repentance for aligning with and operating under the influence of the spirit of death/shadow of death
- Break attachments from the below listed activities and other partnering demonic spirits
- Renounce all of the following activities
- Cast out or evict all partnering evil spirits

Signs: *Fears, Deception, Destruction, Self-destruction such as repeated activities that lead to personal harm or death, Seduction, Nightmares, Mental/Spiritual Torment, Hopelessness, Isolation, Sickness, Thoughts of Suicide/Death*

Unbelief

Fear

Deception

Blinded Heart and Mind

Seduction (luring)
Abortion (one or more)
Discouragement/Hopelessness/Despair/Depression
Sorrow/Aching Heart/Excessive Mourning or Grief
Lethargy
Isolation/Abandons Friends or Family
Occult Involvement involving

Lilith

Diana

Luciferian doctrines

Satan

Wicca practices and rituals especially worship of our Lady and the Lord

Worship of dead saints

Dedication to dead saints

Being named after dead saints

Prayers to dead saints

Ouija board

Occult, witchcraft rituals involving killing of animals or bloodshed

Worship of dead ancestors

Conjuring up the dead

Oppression, Mental Torment

Something keeps whispering that he or she is going to die.

Dreams of:

Being attacked by animals, demons, grim reaper

Being chased by dead people

Being married to dead people

Walking in a graveyard

Being flogged

Being shot

Being hit by a vehicle

Falling into a pit and being unable to get out

Seeing Shadowy Dark Figures

Obsession with Blood, Death, Violence

Sickness or Disease (that does not respond to prayers or medical treatment)

Sharp pains in the body

Sudden loss of appetite

Self-Affliction

Death Wishes, Thoughts of Suicide/Attempts of Suicide

Thoughts of Murder/Murder

Once the house is plundered: command the spirit of death/shadow of death to get out.

- Issue an eviction notice to this spirit (Speak it out loud)

- Loose and welcome in: life and light, prosperity, healing, blessing, a fresh infilling of the Holy Spirit

FAMILIAR SPIRIT: WITCHCRAFT, SPIRIT OF DIVINATION, OCCULT, REBELLION

One day, as we were going to the house of prayer, we encountered a young slave girl who had an evil spirit of divination, the spirit of Python. She had earned great profits for her owners by being a fortune-teller (Acts 16:16 TPT).

Give no regard to mediums and familiar spirits; do not seek after them, to be defiled by them: I am the Lord your God (Leviticus 19:31 NKJV).

For rebellion is as the sin of divination, and insubordination is as iniquity and idolatry (1 Samuel 15:23 NASB).

Bind: *Familiar Spirit and Spirit of Divination/ Occult/Rebellion*

Plunder its house!

- Repentance for aligning with and operating under the influence of the familiar spirit/witchcraft/spirit of divination/occult/rebellion

- Break attachments from the below listed activities and other partnering demonic spirits
- Renounce all of the following activities
- Cast out or evict all partnering evil spirits

Signs: *Independence, Control, Spiritual Error, Fears, OCD, Drugs, Infirmity, Sexual Sin*

Generational Iniquity, Family Curses

Self-Will (independence from God)

Stubbornness, disobedience, rebellion, blasphemy

Control, Manipulation

Lying, deception

Spiritual Error

Unhealthy fear of god or hell

Fear of losing salvation

Superficial spirituality

Religiosity, legalism, ritualism

Doctrinal obsession, doctrinal error

Spiritual adultery, spiritual unfaithfulness

Superstition

Fantasy

Hallucinations

Fears, Suspicions

Obsessions, Compulsion

Drugs (pharmakeia)

Easily Persuaded, Passive Mind

Victim, Lethargy

Poverty Mentality

Entry to Occult

Dungeons and Dragons and other dark games, Ouija board, Pokémon, Anime, Harry Potter, Twilight, horror and "supernatural" movies, all book steeped in witchcraft, occult, vampirism, werewolves and magic; music that defies, mocks or rejects god (hip-hop, rock), astrology, horoscope, tarot cards, tea leaves, fortune telling, palmistry, psychics, past life readings, psychic healing, pendulum divination, charms, fetishes (good luck piece), occult jewelry, yoga, I Ching, martial arts, Rieke (palm healing), video games and online games steeped in the occult, witchcraft, sexual perversion and killing

Occult Activity

Clairvoyance, dreamer (false), divination, channeling, automatic handwriting, mind reading, mental telepathy, false prophesies transcendental meditation, trance, spirit guides hypnosis, mind control, enchanter (spells), charmer, muttering, incantation, white magic, levitation-séance, necromancy (consulting the dead), medium, consulter of the dead, black magic (evil), sorcery (spells, black arts), witch, conjuring (summoning demons), soothsayer, ritualistic body piercing, occult and demonic tattoos, ritualistic flying and suspension by hooks for spiritual enlightenment, Ouija board, physical ritual abuse, death

Cults

Belial, Black Panthers, Buddhism, unbiblical Catholicism, Christian Science, Confucianism, Freemasonry, Eastern Star, Hinduism, Islam, Jehovah's Witnesses (Watchtower), KKK, Mind Control, Mormonism, New Age, Occultism, Rosicrucianism (secret society), Satanism, Scientology, Shintoism, Spiritism, Sufism (Islam-related), Taoism, Theosophy, Unitarianism, Unity, Universalism, Voodoo, Santeria, Wicca, Witchcraft, Lilith worship, Santa Muerte worship, Brujeria

Sexual

Incubus, Succubus (dreams of sexual activity with demon spirits)

Seduction

Incest

Ritual sex

Harlotry (prostitution)

Once the house is plundered: command the familiar spirit/witchcraft/spirit of divination/occult/rebellion to get out.

- Issue an eviction notice to this spirit
  (Speak it out loud)
- Loose and welcome in: truth and revelation, humility, mercy, love, peace, joy, purity, a spirit of prophecy, awakening to the Word of God, awakening of the presence of the Lord, fresh infilling of the Holy Spirit

SPIRIT OF FEAR

For God will never give you the spirit of fear, but the Holy Spirit who gives you mighty power, love, and self-control (2 Timothy 1:7).

Bind: *Spirit of Fear*

Plunder its house!

- Repentance for aligning with and operating under the influence of the spirit of fear
- Break attachments from the below listed activities and other partnering demonic spirits
- Renounce all of the following activities
- Cast out or evict all partnering evil spirits

Signs: *Abandoned, Abused, Fear of Authority, Low Self-Esteem, Unbelief, Depression, Paranoia, Sleep Disorders, Illness, Escape, Addictions, Trauma or Repeated Traumas*

Abandonment

Orphaned

Abuse

Trauma

Fear of Touch

Fear of Giving or Receiving Love

Fear of Authority

Fear of Man

Fear of Confrontation/Correction/Disapproval/
Judgment/Accusation

Fear of Intimidation, Embarrassment

Fear of Failure

Passivity, Timidity, Compromising (conceding)

Frustration

Judging, Resentment

Jealousy

Excessively Self-Aware

    Low self-esteem, inadequacy, inferiority complex,
    insecurity
    Self-Rejection

Unbelief

    Faithlessness, no fellowship with the Father, cannot
    call upon God
    Spiritual blindness, fear of losing salvation, fear of
    God (in an unhealthy way)

Lack of Trust/Doubt/Distrust/Skepticism/Suspicion

Stress/Tension/Anxiety/Apprehension/Worry

Agitation/Vexation/Negativity/Dread

Moodiness, Sorrow, Continual Crying

Loneliness

Depression

Confusion, Ineptness, Paralysis (mental?)
Stuttering
Hyper Sensitivity, Unduly Cautious/Careful
Excitability/Panic/Hysteria
Fears of:

Heights, closed-in places, darkness, germs, danger, death

Phobias, Paranoia, Terror, Torment, Trembling, Rejection
Sleep Disorders

Insomnia, sleeplessness, sleepiness, teeth grinding, nightmares

Sickness

Hormonal imbalance, headaches, high blood pressure, heart attacks, migraines, chronic fatigue syndrome

Escapism

Procrastination
Daydreaming, fantasy, unreality, indifference
Pretension (posing, posturing), sophistication, playacting, theatrics, pouting, hypochondria, isolation, recluse
Restlessness, roving
Self-Reward

Mind Control
Schizophrenia

Insanity

For Fantasy, see also the Spirit of Whoredom

For *Headaches*, see also the Spirit of Infirmity

For *Resentment*, see also the Spirit of Jealousy

Once the house is plundered: command the spirit of fear to get out.

- Issue an eviction notice to this spirit (Speak it out loud)
- Loose and welcome in: humility, mercy, love, peace, joy, a spirit of truth, spirit of boldness, power, love, a sound mind, a spirit of adoption, true kingdom identity, awakening to the Word of God, awakening of the presence of the Lord, fresh infilling of the Holy Spirit

HAUGHTY SPIRIT: PRIDEFUL SPIRIT

An arrogant man is inflated with pride nothing but a snooty scoffer in love with his own opinion. Mr. Mocker is his name! (Proverbs 21:24)

Bind: *Haughty/Prideful Spirit*

Plunder its house!

- Repentance for aligning with and operating under the influence of the haughty/pride spirit
- Break attachments from the below listed activities and other partnering demonic spirits
- Renounce all of the following activities
- Cast out or evict all partnering evil spirits

Signs: *Independence, Intellectualism, Self-Centered, Pride, Control, Entitlement, Anger, Excessively Competitive, Racism*

Competitive (excessively)

Perfectionist

Pride in education, pride in position (excessive)

Entitlement

Coveting, greed, self-pity, idleness

Frustration, Impatience, Agitation

Critical, Judgmental, Resentful, Intolerance, Gossip

Argumentative

Lying/Deception

Spiritual Pride (independence)

Intellectualism (knowledge is from reason),
Rationalism (reason is truth)
Religious spirit, legalism
Rebellion
Rejection of God (atheism)

Ego-Centric

Self-Importance, vanity, self-centered, self-righteous
Self-Delusion, self-deception, selfishness

Pretension (posing or posturing)

False Humility, playacting, theatrics

Uncompassionate (emotionally hard)

Unforgiving

Pride

Superiority, egotism, arrogance, haughtiness,
smugness
Stubborn, obstinate, stiff-necked
Boastful, bragging
Scornful (mocking)
Holier-than-thou attitude, lofty looks

Controlling

Overbearing, domineering, dictatorial

Anger/Bitterness, Bitter Root Judgment/Hatred

Irritability, unkindness

Insolence (rude), contentiousness (combative)

Wrath (anger), rage

Violence

Note: For *Wrath* see also Spirit of Jealousy

Once the house is plundered: command the spirit of pride/haughtiness to get out.

- Issue an eviction notice to this spirit (Speak it out loud)
- Loose and welcome in: humility, mercy, love, peace, joy, a spirit of truth, awakening to the Word of God, awakening of the presence of the Lord, fresh infilling of the Holy Spirit

SPIRIT OF HEAVINESS/DEPRESSION

To grant those who mourn in Zion, giving them a garland instead of ashes, the oil of gladness instead of mourning, the mantle of praise instead of a spirit of fainting. So they will be called oaks of righteousness, the planting of the Lord, that He may be glorified (Isaiah 61:3 NASB).

Bind: *Spirit of Heaviness/Depression*

Plunder its house!

- Repentance for aligning with and operating under the influence of the spirit of heaviness/depression
- Break attachments from the below listed activities and other partnering demonic spirits
- Renounce all of the following activities
- Cast out or evict all partnering evil spirits

Signs: *Abandonment, Rejection, Brokenhearted, Condemnation, Unworthiness, Self-Pity, Hopelessness, Insomnia, Torment, Passivity, Escape, Thoughts of Suicide, Trauma or Repeated Traumas*

Abandonment

   Rejection
   Bastard (to alienate)
   Abortion (having one, surviving one)

Brokenhearted

   Heartbreak, heartache, hurt, inner hurts
   Excessive mourning, grief, sorrow, continual sadness
   Continual Crying

Condemnation/Guilt/False Guilt
Burdened/False Burden, Pressured
Introspection

   Critical, disgust
   Unworthiness, shame

Troubled Spirit, Wounded Spirit
Self-Pity
Lack, Poverty
Discouragement

   Dejection, defeatism
   Despair, despondency, gloom
   Hopelessness
   Dread

Passivity

   Weariness, sleepiness, tiredness, fatigue
   Lethargy, listless, laziness
   Indifference

Insomnia

Torment

Escape

    Isolation, loneliness

    Drivenness (excessive)

    Hyperactivity

    Restlessness, vagabond, wanderer

    Gluttony

    Disorder

    Cruelty

    Suicide

Morbidity (injury, illness)

    Pain, headache, sickness

    Death

Once the house is plundered: command the spirit of heaviness/depression to get out.

- Issue an eviction notice to this spirit (Speak it out loud)
- Loose and welcome in: The Comforter, a garment of praise, joy, love, peace, power, a sound mind, acceptance, true kingdom identity, a fresh infilling of the Holy Spirit, right brain alignment and thoughts

SPIRIT OF INFIRMITY

And behold, there was a woman who had a spirit of infirmity eighteen years and was bent over and could in no way raise herself up (Luke 13:11 NKJV).

Bind: *Spirit of Infirmity*

Plunder its house!

- Repentance for aligning with and operating under the influence of the spirit of infirmity
- Break attachments from the below listed activities and other partnering demonic spirits
- Renounce all of the following activities
- Cast out or evict all partnering evil spirits

Signs: *Unforgiveness, Allergies, Infections, Diseases, Disorders, Mental Illness, Oppression, Death*

Generational Curses

Wounded Spirit

    Unforgiveness

    Bitterness, hatred

Allergies

Hay fever, other allergies

Infections

Fever, inflammation

Colds, bronchitis

Fungus infections

Plague

Venereal disease

Diseases/Chronic Diseases

Arthritis

Asthma

Cancer

Epilepsy, seizures

Heart disorder, heart attack

Skin disorders

Ulcers

Lingering Disorders

ADD, ADHD

Bent body or spine

Bleeding

Blindness

Deafness

Chronic weakness, feebleness

Fainting

Headaches, migraines

Impotence

Lameness, paralysis

Lingering trauma

Mental Illness

Memory loss, senility

Tourette's syndrome

Hallucinations

Schizophrenia paranoia

Mania (obsession, hysteria)

Insanity, lunatic, madness

Spirit of Death

Oppression

Slavery (enslavement, bondage, oppression)

Torment

Death

Note: For *Oppression* **see also Spirit of Heaviness**

For occult activity and cults that lead to infirmity, see Familiar Spirit

Once the house is plundered: command the spirit of infirmity to get out.

- Issue an eviction notice to this spirit (Speak it out loud)
- Loose and welcome in: wholeness, health, life, joy, power, love a sound mind, peace, fresh infilling of the Holy Spirit

SPIRIT OF JEALOUSY

And if a spirit (sense, attitude) of jealousy comes over him and he is jealous and angry at his wife who has defiled herself—or if a spirit of jealousy comes over him and he is jealous of his wife when she has not defiled herself (Numbers 5:14 AMP).

Bind: *Spirit of Jealousy*

Plunder its house!

- Repentance for aligning with and operating under the influence of the spirit of jealousy
- Break attachments from the below listed activities and other partnering demonic spirits
- Renounce all of the following activities
- Cast out or evict all partnering evil spirits

Signs: *Unworthiness, Insecurity, Self-Centered, Competitive, Critical, Anger, Unforgiveness, Argumentative, Gossip, Inability to Cry, Causing Division, Rebellion, Self-Hatred, Bitterness, Hatred, Racism*

Unworthiness, Inferiority

Insecurity

Materialistic/Covetous/Envy/Greed

Dreamer (imaginations)

Ego-Centric/Self-Centered (self-focused)

    Competitive (excessively)

    Discontent, dissatisfaction, restlessness

    Indifference, hardness of heart, inability to cry

    Selfish

Critical

    Judging, faultfinding

    Distrust, suspicion

    Gossip, accusations, backbiting, belittling

Anger

    Spite, (anger), strife (anger), temper, burn (anger), rage

    Bitterness, bitter root judgment, hatred, enmity (hatred)

Unforgiveness

Factiousness (division)

    Seeking to cause debates, causing divisions, disputes

    Contentious, argumentative, bickering, quarreling

    Mocking, dishonorable words, cursing, coarse jesting

    slander, lying

Deception (deceived, deceiving)

Rebellion

Blasphemy

Malice (evil intent, anger)

Retaliation, revenge

Stealing

Fighting, gangs, violence

Cruelty, hurt, sadism (inflicting pain)

Wickedness

Destruction

Murder

Self-Hatred, Suicide

Once the house is plundered: command the spirit of jealousy to get out.

- Issue an eviction notice to this spirit
  (Speak it out loud)
- Loose and welcome in: love, acceptance, peace, joy, self- control, patience, contentment, fresh infilling of the Holy Spirit

LYING SPIRIT

There are six things which the Lord hates, yes, seven which are an abomination to Him: haughty eyes, a lying tongue, and hands that shed innocent blood, a heart that devises wicked plans, feet that run rapidly to evil, a false witness who utters lies, and one who spreads strife among brothers (Proverbs 6:16-19 NASB).

Bind: *Lying Spirit*

Plunder its house!

- Repentance for aligning with and operating under the influence of the lying spirit
- Break attachments from the below listed activities and other partnering demonic spirits
- Renounce all of the following activities
- Cast out or evict all partnering evil spirits

Signs: *Independence, Pride, Performance, Low Self-Image, Poverty, Emotionalism, Wickedness, Rationalization (excuse), False Spirituality Mind Control, Sexual Sin, Drugs, ADD*

Fear of Authority, Other Fears

Independence

Pride, arrogance, vanity

Entitlement

Self-Protection

Performance

Perfectionism, drivenness

Seeking approval

Insecurity, low self-image

False responsibility, false burden

Lying

Excessive talking

Flattery

False compassion

Exaggeration, insinuations (implying)

Gossip, accusations, slander

False witness

Deceit, cheating, manipulation

Stealing, robbery

Rationalization (excuse)

Hypocrisy

Poverty, Financial Problems (especially tithing)

Emotionalism

Passion (inordinate)

Crying

Arguments
Profanity
Wickedness
Vengeance

Religious Spirit

Jezebel Spirit

False Spirituality

False Prophet/False Prophecy

Dreamer, Vain Imaginations/Strong Delusions

Superstitions

False Oaths

Curses, Self-Inflicted Curses

False Teaching/False Doctrines/Heresy

Divination

Mind Control

Mental Bondage

Sexual

Fantasies, uncleanness, lust, pornography, compulsive masturbation, fornication, adultery, sodomy, lesbianism, homosexual behavior, transsexual behavior, transvestite, depraved desires

Drugs

Notes: For *False Prophecy,* see also Familiar Spirit.

For "homosexuality" and *Sodomy,* see also Spirit of Perversion, Whoredom.

Once the house is plundered: command the lying spirit to get out.

- Issue an eviction notice to this spirit
  (Speak it out loud)
- Loose and welcome in: honesty, goodness, truth, purity, joy, awakening to the Word of God, a fresh filling of the Holy Spirit

SPIRIT OF ERROR

We are of God. He who knows God hears us; he who is not of God does not hear us. By this we know the spirit of truth and the spirit of error (1 John 4:6 NKJV).

Bind: *Spirit of Error*

Plunder its house!

- Repentance for aligning with and operating under the influence of the spirit of error
- Break attachments from the below listed activities and other partnering demonic spirits
- Renounce all of the following activities
- Cast out or evict all partnering evil spirits

Signs: *Lack of Discernment, Easily Persuaded, False Beliefs, Pride, Anger, Competition, Lies*

Lack of Discernment

Easily Persuaded (toward error)

False Doctrines, New Age Beliefs

  Cults, occult, doctrines of devils

Pride/Haughtiness

Always right, unsubmissive, unteachable

Angry

Argumentative, defensive, contentious, (self-protection)
Hatred

Competition (excessive)

Hypocrisy, Lies

Once the house is plundered: command the spirit of error to get out.

- Issue an eviction notice to this spirit
  (Speak it out loud)
- Loose and welcome in: Spirit of Truth,
  Spirit of Promise, patience, peace,
  self-control

SPIRIT OF PERVERSION/WHOREDOM/ LUST/SEXUAL SIN

The Lord has mingled a perverse spirit in her;
so they have caused Egypt to err in her every
work (Isaiah 19:14 MEV).

Bind: *Spirit of Perversion/Lust, Spirit of Whoredom/ Sexual Sin*

Plunder its house!

- Repentance for aligning with and operating under the influence of the spirit of perversion/whoredom/lust/sexual sin
- Break attachments from the below listed activities and other partnering demonic spirits
- Renounce all of the following activities
- Cast out or evict all partnering evil spirits

Signs: *Lusts, Sexual Sin, Emotional Dissatisfaction, Wounded Spirit, Confusion, Unbelief, Deception, Worldliness, Evil Actions*

Wounded Spirit

Guilt, shame, chronic worry
Emotional weakness, weakness, dizziness
Emotional dissatisfaction

Unforgiveness

Hatred

Self-hatred, marking, cutting, suicidal thoughts, actions

Doubt, Unbelief

Atheism

Idolatry

False teachings

Doctrinal error (twisting the word of God)

Diviner (false prophet)

Confusion (spirit of Egypt)

Deception

Lover of Self

Arrogance, stubbornness, contentiousness, crankiness

Lust for Authority/Power/Position/Social Standing

Lust for Money, Greed, Hoarding, Poverty

Lust for Food

Lust for Activity (excessive)

Worldliness

Foolishness

Drunkard spirit

Tattoos

Evil actions

Cruelty

Lust for Sex

Uncontrollable sexual desires, perverse sexual acts, sensuality, lustful fantasy, filthy mindedness, adulterous fantasy, pornography, self-gratification, compulsive masturbation, self-exposure, exhibitionism
Seduction

Fornication (sexual activity before marriage), Promiscuity, Unfaithfulness, Adultery, Rape

Harlotry, whoredom, prostitution of body, soul or spirit; illegitimate children, bastard spirit (unholy covenant)
Abortion
sexual deviation, perversion
Homosexuality (same sex), sodomy (anal, oral), lesbianism (same sex)

Bisexuality (with both sexes), Transvestite (cross-dressing+),

Sadomasochism (physical, mental suffering in sex)
Incest (family members)
Child abuse
Pedophilia (with children)
Incubus, Succubus (dreams of sex with spirits)
Chronic sexual dissatisfaction, frigidity

Seducing spirit, Spirits of Shame, Pride, Lust

Once the house is plundered: command the spirit of perversion/whoredom/lust/sexual sin to get out.

- Issue an eviction notice to this spirit (Speak it out loud)
- Loose and welcome in: chastity, discernment, godliness, purity, Spirit of Truth, Spirit of Holiness, ability to abstain from sexual sin, self-control, healing from addiction and bondage

SEDUCING SPIRIT

But the [Holy] Spirit explicitly and unmistakably declares that in later times some will turn away from the faith, paying attention instead to deceitful and seductive spirits and doctrines of demons (1 Timothy 4:1 AMP).

Bind: *Seducing Spirit*

Plunder its house!

- Repentance for aligning with and operating under the influence of the seducing spirit
- Break attachments from the below listed activities and other partnering demonic spirits
- Renounce all of the following activities
- Cast out or evict all partnering evil spirits

Signs: *Fear of Man, Seeks Attention, Dulled Sense of Right and Wrong, Attracted to False Prophets, Evil Persons, Greed, Hypocrisy*

Fear of Man

Wanders from the Truth of God

Seared Conscience (dulled sense of right and wrong)

Emulation (imitates)
Gullible/Easily Swayed/Easily Deceived/Enticed/Seduced
Attracted to False Prophets, Signs and Wonders
Fascination with Evil Ways

Evil objects, Evil persons
Music that defies, mocks or rejects God
Trance
Including fascination with evil television shows and movies steeped in the occult, vampires, dark angels, werewolves, etc.

Seeks Attention
Sensual in Dress, Actions
Greed, Exploitation
Hypocritical Lies

Once the house is plundered: command the seducing spirit to get out.

- Issue an eviction notice to this spirit (Speak it out loud)
- Loose and welcome in: Spirit of Truth, Spirit of Holiness, purity, awakening to the truth and Word of God, true gift of prophecy

Spirit of Slumber/Unbelief

God granted them a spirit of deep slumber.
He closed their eyes to the truth and prevented
their ears from hearing up to this day
(Romans 11:8).

Bind: *Spirit of Slumber/Unbelief*

Plunder its house!

- Repentance for aligning with and operating under the influence of the spirit of slumber/unbelief
- Break attachments from the below listed activities and other partnering demonic spirits
- Renounce all of the following activities
- Cast out or evict all partnering evil spirits

Signs: *Can't Hear or Understand the Word of God, Unbelief, Confusion, Distracted, Mental Slowness, Sleep Disorders, Sickness, Sexual Sin*

Can't Hear the Word of God
Can't Stay Awake in Church
Confusion
Distracted Easily
ADD, ADHD

Dizziness

Mental Slowness

Lethargy

Lazy

Sleep Disorders

Sleepiness, chronic fatigue syndrome, sleeplessness

Unbelief, Blasphemer

Fear, Torment, Terror

Sexual Sin, Perversions

Sickness

Eye disorders, blindness

Hearing problems

Arthritis

Asthma

Anemia

Circulatory problems

Palpitations

Note: For *Sickness* see also Spirit of Infirmity

Once the house is plundered: command the spirit of slumber/unbelief to get out.

- Issue an eviction notice to this spirit (Speak it out loud)

- Loose and welcome in: being filled with the Spirit, spiritual eyes open, healing, awakening to the Word of God, awakening to the presence of God

SPIRIT OF REJECTION

Bind: *Spirit of Rejection*

Plunder its house!

- Repentance for aligning with and operating under the influence of the spirit of rejection
- Break attachments from the below listed activities and other partnering demonic spirits
- Renounce all of the following activities
- Cast out or evict all partnering evil spirits

Signs: *Self-Rejection, Overly Aggressive Reactions, Independence, Self-Idolatry, Covetousness, Pride, Sabotaging of Relationships, Fears, Rebellion, Emotional Immaturity, Trauma or Repeated Traumas*

Aggressive Reactions

Refusing comfort
Rejections of others
Harshness, hardness
Skepticism, unbelief
Aggressive attitudes
Swearing, foul language
Argumentative
Stubborn, defiance

Rebellion

Fighting

Self-Rejection

Low self-image

Inferiorities

Insecurity

Inadequacy

Sadness, grief, sorrow

Self-accusation, self-condemnation

Inability or refusal to communicate

Fear of failure

Fear of other's opinions

Anxiety, worry, depression

Negativity, pessimism

Hopelessness, despair

Measures to Counter Fear of Rejection

Striving, Achievement

Performance, Competition

Withdrawal, Aloneness

Independence:

Isolation

Self-protection

Self-centeredness

Selfishness

Self-justification

Self-righteousness

Self-Idolatry:

Criticism

Judgment

Envy, jealousy

Covetousness

Self-pity

Pride:

Egotism

Haughtiness

Arrogance

Manipulation

Possessiveness

Emotional immaturity

Perfectionism

Once the house is plundered: command the spirit of rejection to get out.

- Issue an eviction notice to this spirit (Speak it out loud)
- Loose and welcome in: love, acceptance, true kingdom identity, spirit of adoption, awakening to the Father heart of God

RELIGIOUS SPIRIT

Jesus spoke up and said, "Watch out for the yeast of the Pharisees and the Sadducees" (Matthew 16:6).

Bind: *Religious Spirit*

Plunder its house!

- Repentance for aligning with and operating under the influence of the religious spirit
- Break attachments from the below listed activities and other partnering demonic spirits
- Renounce all of the following activities
- Cast out or evict all partnering evil spirits

Signs: *Legalism, Pride, Holier-Than-Thou Attitude, Ritual over Relationship, Fear, Judgment, Against New Moves of God*

Overemphasis on Outward Form

Have to say the right word
Have to do the right things
Have to have the right look
Fear of what others think
Dresses to attract attention on oneself

Dresses like Jesus, an angel, in a manner that draws attention to the person and not to Jesus

Acts otherworldly

Always quoting scripture, cannot engage in conversation without making everything spiritual, acting above others

False tongues

Condemnation and Fear

Condemns when things aren't done "just right"

Perfectionism

Fear of failure

Fear of losing man's approval

Pride

Judgmental

Critical

Holier-than-thou attitude

Self-righteous

Self-exalting or great false humility

Functions closely with a political mindset and spirit

Resists New Moves of God

Jealousy

Steeped in tradition

Speaks out against moves of the Lord

Their tradition and movement is the most spiritual and elite

Elitist thinking about their traditions

Superstition

With using the Word
With their rituals
All tradition works and fear based

Oppressive Legalism

No flexibility
Rigid dogma
Required and method-based prayers
Required and method-based services
No freedom for gifts or the Holy Spirit to move freely
No thriving relationship with Jesus or the Holy Spirit

Driven Need to Figure Out God

Intellectualism
Driven to make God predictable
Cannot relate to the supernatural
Places God in a box
Much doctrinal error
Deception
Lying spirit

Dependence on Self-Effort

Achieves righteousness through works of the flesh
Striving
Cannot experience peace separate from works
Perfectionist

Undue Emphasis on Tradition

Turning tradition into an idol

Idol worship

Worship focused toward an object or person and not to Jesus

No spiritual life or presence on the tradition

Spiritually dead

Accuses and condemns those who do not embrace tradition

Falsely honoring God with words, but not in heart and action

Spirit of Unbelief

Spirit of Slumber

Spirit of Bondage

Spirit of Fear

Once the house is plundered: command the religious spirit to get out.

- Issue an eviction notice to this spirit (Speak it out loud)
- Loose and welcome in: Spirit of Truth, freedom, relationship with Jesus, awakening to His Word, awakening to His presence, fresh infilling of the Holy Spirit

SPIRIT OF JEZEBEL

But I have this against you: you tolerate that woman Jezebel, who calls herself a prophetess and is seducing my loving servants. She is teaching that it is permissible to indulge in sexual immorality and to eat food sacrificed to idols. I have waited for her to repent from her vile immorality, but she refuses to do so. Now I will lay her low with terrible distress along with all her adulterous partners if they do not repent (Revelation 2:20-22).

Bind: *The Spirit of Jezebel (This spirit can operate in both men and women)*

Plunder its house!

- Repentance for aligning with and operating under the influence of the Jezebel spirit
- Break attachments from the below listed activities and other partnering demonic spirits
- Renounce all of the following activities
- Cast out or evict all partnering evil spirits

Signs: *Prophetic (but wants to control those who are truly prophetic); Gets Close to Leadership, Defensive, Not Teachable, Bypasses Proper Authority, Deceptive, Spiritual Pride, Desires Control; In the World: Seductive, Power Hungry (makes evil deals for power, will say one thing to gain favor will do the exact opposite to get power)*

Prophetic Assignment

Appears prophetic

Threatened by true prophets

Speaks soulish prophecies to entice people

Controls those who are true prophets

Silences the voice of the true prophet

Steals favor from the true prophet

False Favor

Establishes relationship with leader

Finds weakness and uses against others, leaders

Usurps authority for complete control

Seduction with words

Seduction with actions

Seeks to gain pastoral, leadership endorsement

Manipulation

Seeks recognition impurely

Will deceive and lie to gain favor (lying spirit)

Operates in false humility (for the sake of favor)

Will look for the weak link (someone to become the Ahab)

Appears Very Spiritual

Uses flattery to appeal to others

Their word is the final word even over leaders

Operates in a religious spirit

Quick to point out faults of others while appearing sad about those faults

Doctrinal error, subtle twisting of the Word of God

Impure motives

Seek disciples to lead

Very secretive when praying for others (usually in isolated places)

Says to be able to impart a higher spiritual impartation than anyone else

Control

Controls prayer, church, Christian meetings

Business meetings

Governmental meetings

In the world wants media attention

Will engage in evil deeds to control

Sexual acts

Sexual perversion

Mammon, greed/illegal money dealings for wealth

Lies and Defames for Power/Control

Kills

Robs Inheritance

Pride

Control

False humility

Actually, has poor self- esteem, wears religious mask to hide it

Will engage in very overt "spiritual acts" to gain attention

Wailing, crying, mourning, warring, contending, prophesying

Families Life Is Shaky

When in the World, Often Involved in Occult Activity

Once the house is plundered: command the spirit of Jezebel to get out.

- Issue an eviction notice to this spirit (Speak it out loud)
- Loose and welcome in: Spirit of Truth, love, spirit of prophecy, holiness, purity, new infilling of the Holy Spirit, awakening to His Word and awakening to His presence

I spent many years learning deliverance ministry from Eddie and Alice Smith. Portions of this list are from the wisdom they achieved over years of engaging in deliverance ministry. As we continue to move forward in this ministry we also have received further revelation concerning the demonic spirits we are dealing with on a regular basis. This is not an exhaustive list. As we continue to gain further revelation and understanding we continue to add revisions to this list. The portions that we learned from the Smith are used by permission.[1]

NOTE

1. Alice Smith, *Delivering the Captives* (Bloomington, MN: Bethany House Publishers, 2006), 96-118, Used by permission of publisher.

ABOUT REBECCA GREENWOOD

Rebecca Greenwood co-founded Christian Harvest International, Strategic Prayer Apostolic Network and Christian Harvest Training Center which ministers to the nations through teaching at Christian conferences, schools and gatherings and travels extensively releasing prophetic words and strategies for cities, regions, nations, and spheres of influence. Over the past 30 years, she has mobilized and led prophetic intercession and transformational spiritual warfare prayer journeys to over 45 nations and within spheres of government which have resulted in effective transformational breakthrough. She is the author of ten books. And is the host of Reigning in Life which appears on It's Supernatural Network (ISN). Rebecca and her husband, Greg, reside in Colorado Springs, CO, and they have three beautiful daughters and three wonderful sons-in-law. Visit www.christianharvestintl.org to request Rebecca to speak at an event, for further resources and to access her ministry schedule.

NOTES

NOTES

NOTES

NOTES

NOTES

NOTES

NOTES

NOTES

NOTES

NOTES